Contents

1.	Introduction	1
2.	Listen Actively	3
3.	Empathize with Customers	8
4.	Train Employees Thoroughly	14
5.	Respond Promptly	21
6.	Personalize Interactions	28
7.	Seek Feedback	35
8.	Use Positive Language	42
9.	Be Accessible	49
10.	Follow Up	56
11.	Empower Employees	64
12.	Create a Knowledge Base	72
13.	Maintain a Positive Attitude	80
14.	Offer Proactive Support	88
15.	Show Appreciation	96
16.	Handle Complaints Gracefully	104

Introduction

In today's hyper-connected world, where customers have more choices than ever before, exceptional customer service is not just a nice-to-have—it's a critical differentiator. Companies that consistently deliver outstanding service create loyal customers, generate positive word-of-mouth, and build a reputation that sets them apart from the competition. But what does it take to truly maximize customer service? How can businesses go beyond meeting expectations to delighting and surprising their customers at every turn?

This book is your comprehensive guide to mastering the art of customer service. Whether you're a small business owner, a customer service manager, or an executive looking to enhance your organization's customer-centric culture, this book will equip you with the strategies, insights, and practical tools you need to elevate your customer service to new heights.

We'll explore the core principles of exceptional service, delve into real-world examples of companies that have excelled in this area, and provide actionable steps you can take to create memorable experiences for your customers. From building a customer-first mindset to leveraging technology for seamless service delivery, this book covers every aspect of what it takes to turn customer interactions into powerful opportunities for growth and success.

Join us on a journey to discover how maximizing customer service can transform your business, foster deep connections with your customers, and ultimately, drive long-term success. Whether you're just starting out or looking to refine your existing approach, the insights and strategies in this book will help you unlock the full potential of exceptional customer service.

Listen Actively

Active listening is a fundamental aspect of effective communication, especially in customer service. It involves fully concentrating, understanding, responding, and remembering what the customer is saying. Here's a detailed explanation of how active listening can significantly enhance customer service:

1. Building Trust and Rapport

Why it Matters:

When customers feel heard and understood, it builds trust. Trust is the cornerstone of any relationship, including the one between a business and its customers.

How Active Listening Helps:

Demonstrates Empathy: Actively listening shows that you care about the customer's issues and value their input.

Encourages Openness: Customers are more likely to share honest feedback and concerns when they feel their opinions are valued.

2. Accurate Understanding of Customer Needs

Why it Matters:

Misunderstanding a customer's needs can lead to frustration and dissatisfaction.

How Active Listening Helps:

Clarifies Issues: By paying close attention, service representatives can accurately identify the root of the customer's problem.

Reduces Errors: Ensures that the right solution is provided, minimizing mistakes and the need for follow-up corrections.

3. Enhanced Problem Solving

Why it Matters:

Effective problem-solving directly impacts customer satisfaction and loyalty.

How Active Listening Helps:

Gathers Detailed Information: Active listening allows the representative to gather all necessary details to address the issue comprehensively.

Facilitates Tailored Solutions: Enables personalized solutions that better meet the specific needs of the customer.

4. Improving Customer Satisfaction

Why it Matters:

Satisfied customers are more likely to return, recommend the business, and provide positive feedback.

How Active Listening Helps:

Creates Positive Experiences: Customers appreciate being listened to, which enhances their overall experience.

Reduces Frustration: Quickly understanding and addressing concerns reduces the time and effort a customer has to invest in resolving their issues.

5. Enhancing Communication

Why it Matters:

Clear and effective communication prevents misunderstandings and ensures that both the customer and the representative are on the same page.

How Active Listening Helps:

Encourages Effective Dialogue: Allows for a two-way conversation where both parties feel heard and understood.

Prevents Miscommunication: Ensures that the representative accurately understands and conveys information.

6. Promoting Continuous Improvement

Why it Matters:

Customer feedback is crucial for identifying areas for improvement within a business.

How Active Listening Helps:

Gathers Valuable Insights: By listening to customers, businesses can gain insights into common issues and areas needing improvement.

Informs Training and Development: Helps in identifying training needs for staff based on common themes or issues raised by customers.

7. **Fostering a Positive Company Culture**

Why it Matters:

A culture that prioritizes listening and understanding can improve employee satisfaction and performance.

How Active Listening Helps:

Encourages a Supportive Environment: Employees who feel heard by management are more likely to feel valued and motivated.

Promotes Collaboration: Active listening within teams can improve communication and collaboration, leading to better overall customer service.

Techniques for Active Listening:

Maintain Eye Contact: Shows attentiveness and respect.

Nod and Provide Feedback: Simple gestures and verbal affirmations like "I see" or "I understand" indicate that you are following the conversation.

Paraphrase and Summarize: Repeat back what the customer has said to ensure understanding and show that you are engaged.

Ask Open-Ended Questions: Encourages the customer to provide more detailed information.

Avoid Interrupting: Let the customer finish their thoughts before responding.

Show Empathy: Acknowledge the customer's feelings and frustrations.

To Conclude:

By integrating active listening into customer service practices, businesses can create more meaningful interactions, resolve issues more efficiently, and build stronger, more loyal customer relationships.

Empathizing With Customers

Empathizing with customers is a crucial element in delivering exceptional customer service. Empathy involves understanding and sharing the feelings of another person, which in the context of customer service means truly comprehending the customer's concerns, frustrations, and needs. Here's a detailed explanation of how empathizing with customers helps to improve customer service:

1. Building Stronger Customer Relationships

Why it Matters:

Strong relationships with customers are the foundation of customer loyalty and satisfaction.

How Empathy Helps:

Creates Connection: When customers feel understood, they are more likely to feel connected to the business.

Fosters Trust: Empathetic interactions build trust, making customers feel valued and respected.

2. Enhancing Customer Satisfaction

Why it Matters:

Satisfied customers are more likely to return and recommend the business to others.

How Empathy Helps:

Addresses Emotional Needs: Recognizing and addressing the emotional aspects of a customer's issue can lead to higher satisfaction.

Positive Experiences: Empathy contributes to positive customer experiences, even if the issue isn't resolved immediately.

3. Improving Problem Resolution

Why it Matters:

Effective and efficient problem resolution is key to maintaining customer satisfaction.

How Empathy Helps:

Understanding the Root Cause: Empathizing allows customer service representatives to better understand the true nature of the problem.

Tailored Solutions: Empathetic listening leads to more personalized and effective solutions that meet the specific needs of the customer.

4. Reducing Customer Frustration

Why it Matters:

Frustrated customers are more likely to leave negative reviews and take their business elsewhere.

How Empathy Helps:

Calms Tensions: Acknowledging a customer's feelings can help to de-escalate tense situations.

Shows Care: Demonstrating empathy shows that the company cares about the customer's experience and is committed to resolving their issues.

5. Enhancing Communication

Why it Matters:

Clear and compassionate communication is essential for effective customer service.

How Empathy Helps:

Encourages Open Dialogue: Customers are more likely to communicate openly when they feel understood.

Clarifies Understanding: Empathetic responses often include paraphrasing and summarizing, which helps clarify the issue and ensure both parties are on the same page.

6. Promoting Positive Company Image

Why it Matters:

A company known for its empathetic customer service can gain a competitive advantage.

How Empathy Helps:

Boosts Reputation: Word of mouth and reviews often highlight the empathy shown by customer service representatives.

Differentiates the Business: Empathy can set a business apart in industries where customer service is often lacking.

7. Fostering Employee Satisfaction and Performance

Why it Matters:

Happy and motivated employees are crucial for delivering high-quality customer service.

How Empathy Helps:

-Encourages a Supportive Culture: When employees feel valued and understood by their employers, they are more likely to exhibit empathy towards customers.

Reduces Burnout: Understanding and addressing the emotional aspects of customer service can reduce employee stress and burnout.

Techniques for Demonstrating Empathy:

Active Listening: Fully concentrate on what the customer is saying without interrupting.

Acknowledge Feelings: Verbally recognize the customer's emotions, e.g., "I understand that this is frustrating for you."

Use Compassionate Language: Use words and tone that convey understanding and concern.

Share Personal Experiences: When appropriate, share relevant experiences to show understanding.

Follow Up: Check back with customers to ensure their issue was resolved and to show continued concern for their satisfaction.

Practical Examples of Empathy in Customer Service:

Scenario 1: A customer is upset because their order was delivered late.

Empathetic Response: "I understand how frustrating it can be to wait for a delivery that doesn't arrive on time. Let me see what I can do to resolve this for you quickly."

Scenario 2: A customer is confused about how to use a new product.

 - **Empathetic Response:** "I can see how this might be confusing. Let me walk you through the setup process step-by-step to make it easier for you."

In Conclusion:

Empathy in customer service is not just about resolving issues; it's about building meaningful relationships, enhancing customer satisfaction, and creating positive experiences that foster loyalty. By training employees to empathize with customers, businesses can significantly improve their customer service and overall reputation. Empathy transforms a simple transaction into a connection, making customers feel valued and understood, which is the cornerstone of excellent customer service.

Training Employees Thoroughly

Thoroughly training employees is essential for delivering outstanding customer service. Comprehensive training equips employees with the necessary skills, knowledge, and confidence to effectively interact with customers, resolve issues, and represent the company positively. Here's a detailed explanation of how thoroughly training employees improves customer service:

1. Enhanced Product and Service Knowledge

Why it Matters:

Customers expect accurate and detailed information about products and services. Inaccurate or insufficient information can lead to customer frustration and loss of trust.

How Training Helps:

Comprehensive Understanding: Employees gain a deep understanding of the company's offerings, enabling them to provide accurate information and answer customer questions competently.

Confidence in Communication: Well-trained employees can communicate more confidently and effectively, enhancing the customer's experience.

2. Improved Problem-Solving Skills

Why it Matters:

Efficiently resolving customer issues is critical to maintaining customer satisfaction and loyalty.

How Training Helps:

Identifying Solutions: Training equips employees with the skills to identify and implement effective solutions quickly.

Handling Complex Issues: Employees learn strategies for dealing with more complex or uncommon problems, reducing the need for escalation and ensuring a faster resolution.

3. Consistency in Customer Service

Why it Matters:

Consistency ensures that all customers receive the same high level of service, regardless of which employee they interact with.

How Training Helps:

Standardized Procedures: Training ensures all employees follow the same procedures and guidelines, providing a uniform customer experience.

Unified Approach: Employees are trained on the company's service philosophy and standards, ensuring a cohesive approach to customer service.

4. Enhanced Communication Skills

Why it Matters:

Effective communication is key to understanding and addressing customer needs.

How Training Helps:

Active Listening: Training emphasizes the importance of listening to customers, ensuring their concerns are fully understood before responding.

Clear and Positive Language: Employees learn to use clear, positive, and professional language, which helps in delivering messages effectively and maintaining a positive tone.

5. Increased Customer Satisfaction

Why it Matters:

Satisfied customers are more likely to return, make repeat purchases, and recommend the company to others.

How Training Helps:

Personalized Service: Training enables employees to tailor their service to individual customer needs, enhancing the overall experience.

Efficient Service: Well-trained employees can handle inquiries and issues more efficiently, reducing wait times and increasing satisfaction.

6. Empowered Employees

Why it Matters:

Empowered employees are more confident in their roles and more capable of providing exceptional service.

How Training Helps:

Decision-Making Skills: Training programs often include scenarios that help employees develop their decision-making skills, allowing them to handle situations independently and confidently.

Increased Autonomy: Employees who feel well-prepared are more likely to take initiative and go above and beyond for customers.

7. Better Handling of Difficult Situations

Why it Matters:

Difficult situations, such as dealing with angry or frustrated customers, require specific skills and strategies.

How Training Helps:

Conflict Resolution: Training provides techniques for de-escalating conflicts and managing difficult conversations effectively.

Maintaining Professionalism: Employees learn how to remain calm and professional, even under pressure, which helps in resolving issues more effectively and leaving customers with a positive impression.

8. Promoting a Positive Company Image

Why it Matters:

The quality of customer service reflects directly on the company's brand and reputation.

How Training Helps:

Brand Representation: Employees who are well-trained in the company's values and mission can better represent the brand.

Positive Interactions: Consistently positive interactions with knowledgeable and helpful employees enhance the company's reputation.

9. Increased Employee Satisfaction and Retention

Why it Matters:

Satisfied employees are more likely to stay with the company, reducing turnover and maintaining a stable, experienced workforce.

How Training Helps:

Career Development: Providing thorough training shows employees that the company invests in their development, which can increase job satisfaction and loyalty.

Confidence and Morale: Employees who feel capable and confident in their roles are more satisfied and motivated, which translates into better customer service.

10. Continuous Improvement

Why it Matters:

Ongoing improvement in customer service is necessary to meet changing customer expectations and stay competitive.

How Training Helps:

Adaptability: Continuous training ensures employees are up-to-date with the latest industry trends, tools, and best practices.

Feedback Implementation: Training programs can incorporate customer feedback to address areas of improvement and refine service strategies.

In Conclusion

Thoroughly training employees is a strategic investment that pays off in numerous ways. It equips employees with the necessary knowledge and skills to provide high-quality service, enhances their confidence and satisfaction, and ensures consistency across all customer interactions. By prioritizing comprehensive training, companies can significantly improve their customer service, leading to higher customer satisfaction, loyalty, and a positive brand reputation.

Responding Properly

Responding promptly to customer inquiries and issues is a critical component of excellent customer service. Prompt responses demonstrate a company's commitment to its customers, help to build trust, and enhance overall customer satisfaction. Here's a detailed explanation of how responding promptly improves customer service:

1. Building Trust and Credibility

Why it Matters:

Customers need to trust that a company will be there when they need help. Prompt responses show that the company is reliable and values its customers' time.

How Prompt Responses Help:

Demonstrates Reliability: Quick responses indicate that the company is dependable and committed to addressing customer needs.

Fosters Trust: When customers receive timely assistance, they are more likely to trust the company and feel secure in their choice.

2. Enhancing Customer Satisfaction

Why it Matters:

Timely responses are crucial in meeting customer expectations. Customers appreciate quick solutions to their problems and value businesses that prioritize their needs.

How Prompt Responses Help:

Meets Expectations: Customers expect quick resolutions, and meeting these expectations leads to higher satisfaction.

Reduces Anxiety: Prompt replies can alleviate customer anxiety and frustration, particularly in urgent situations.

3. Preventing Escalation of Issues

Why it Matters:

Delays in responding can exacerbate customer issues, leading to increased frustration and potentially more complex problems.

How Prompt Responses Help:

Addresses Problems Early: Quickly addressing issues can prevent them from escalating into more serious concerns.

Minimizes Negative Impact: Timely intervention can reduce the likelihood of negative reviews or loss of business.

4. Improving Problem Resolution Efficiency

Why it Matters:

Efficient problem resolution is essential for maintaining customer satisfaction and loyalty.

How Prompt Responses Help:

Streamlines Resolution: Immediate attention to issues often leads to faster and more efficient resolution.

Enhances Productivity: Quick responses keep the workflow moving, allowing more issues to be resolved in less time.

5. Boosting Customer Loyalty and Retention

Why it Matters:

Satisfied customers are more likely to remain loyal and continue doing business with a company.

How Prompt Responses Help:

Creates Positive Experiences: Timely responses contribute to a positive customer experience, encouraging repeat business.

Encourages Recommendations: Customers who experience prompt and effective service are more likely to recommend the company to others.

6. Differentiating from Competitors

Why it Matters:

In competitive markets, exceptional customer service can be a key differentiator.

How Prompt Responses Help:

Stand Out: Quick and efficient customer service sets a company apart from competitors who may be slower to respond.

Builds Reputation: A reputation for prompt service can attract new customers and retain existing ones.

7. Enhancing Communication and Clarity

Why it Matters:

Clear and timely communication is essential for effective customer service.

How Prompt Responses Helps:

Reduces Miscommunication: Prompt responses facilitate clear and continuous communication, reducing the chances of misunderstandings.

Clarifies Expectations: Immediate replies help set clear expectations regarding the resolution process and timelines.

8. Encouraging Customer Feedback

Why it Matters:

Customer feedback is vital for continuous improvement and innovation.

How Prompt Responses Help:

Invites Dialogue: Customers are more likely to provide feedback if they know the company will respond quickly.

Shows Appreciation: Timely responses demonstrate that the company values customer input and is eager to improve.

9. Increasing Efficiency and Workflow Management

Why it Matters:

Efficient workflow management is essential for maintaining high service standards.

How Prompt Responses Help:

Reduces Backlog: Addressing issues as they arise prevents a backlog of unresolved inquiries.

Optimizes Resources: Efficient response times allow for better allocation of resources and management of customer service workloads.#

10. Maintaining a Positive Company Image

Why it Matters:

A company's reputation is significantly influenced by its customer service quality.

How Prompt Responses Help:

Positive Perception: Prompt responses contribute to a positive perception of the company as responsive and customer-centric.

Builds Brand Loyalty: Consistent, timely service helps build a strong, loyal customer base that views the company favourably.

Practical Strategies for Ensuring Prompt Responses:

1. Automated Acknowledgments: Use automated responses to immediately acknowledge customer inquiries and set expectations for a follow-up.

2. Prioritize Urgent Issues: Implement a system for prioritizing urgent or high-impact customer issues.

3. Train Employees: Ensure that customer service representatives are trained to respond quickly and efficiently.

4. Leverage Technology: Utilize customer service software and tools to manage and track inquiries effectively.

5. Set Clear Goals: Establish and monitor response time goals to ensure timely service.

6. Monitor Channels: Regularly monitor all customer service channels (email, chat, social media, etc.) to ensure no inquiries are overlooked.

In Conclusion

Responding promptly to customer inquiries and issues is a cornerstone of excellent customer service. It helps build trust, enhance customer satisfaction, prevent issue escalation, and improve overall problem resolution efficiency. By prioritizing prompt responses, companies can differentiate themselves from competitors, encourage customer loyalty, and maintain a positive brand image. Investing in strategies and tools that enable quick responses is crucial for any business aiming to provide exceptional customer service.

Personal Interactions

Personalizing interactions in customer service is about tailoring the experience to meet the specific needs, preferences, and past interactions of individual customers. This approach can significantly enhance customer satisfaction, loyalty, and overall experience. Here's a detailed explanation of how personalizing interactions helps to improve customer service:

1. Building Stronger Relationships

Why it Matters:

Strong relationships with customers are essential for long-term business success. Personalization makes customers feel valued and appreciated.

How Personalized Interactions Help:

Creates Connection: Personalizing interactions helps to establish a deeper emotional connection with customers, making them feel understood and valued.

Fosters Trust When customers see that a company remembers their preferences and history, it builds trust and strengthens the relationship.

2. Enhancing Customer Satisfaction

Why it Matters:

Customers are more satisfied when their specific needs and preferences are acknowledged and met.

How Personalized Interactions Help:

Meets Individual Needs: By tailoring the service to individual needs, companies can provide more relevant and satisfying experiences.

Shows Care and Attention: Personalization demonstrates that the company cares about the customer's unique situation, leading to higher satisfaction levels.

3. Improving Problem Resolution

Why it Matters:

Effective and efficient problem resolution is crucial for maintaining customer satisfaction.

How Personalized Interactions Help:

Contextual Solutions: Understanding a customer's history and preferences allows for more accurate and effective problem-solving.

Quick Identification of Issues: Personalized interactions can help service representatives quickly identify recurring issues and provide faster resolutions.

4. Increasing Customer Loyalty and Retention

Why it Matters:

Loyal customers are more likely to make repeat purchases and recommend the business to others.

How Personalized Interactions Help:

Encourages Repeat Business: Customers are more likely to return to a company that treats them as individuals rather than just another number.

Builds Loyalty: Personalized service fosters a sense of loyalty as customers feel a stronger connection to the brand.

5. Creating Positive Customer Experiences

Why it Matters:

Positive experiences lead to higher customer satisfaction and positive word-of-mouth.

How Personalized Interactions Help:

Enhances the Experience: Tailored interactions make the customer experience more enjoyable and memorable.

Increases Engagement: Customers are more engaged and responsive when the interaction feels personal and relevant to them.

6. Differentiating from Competitors

Why it Matters:

In competitive markets, exceptional customer service can be a key differentiator.

How Personalized Interactions Help:

Stand Out: Personalized service can set a company apart from competitors who offer more generic customer service.

Builds Brand Identity: A reputation for personalized service strengthens the brand identity and attracts more customers.

7. Encouraging Customer Feedback

Why it Matters:

Customer feedback is vital for continuous improvement and innovation.

How Personalized Interactions Help:

-Invites Open Communication: Customers are more likely to provide honest feedback when they feel personally valued.

Gathers Insightful Data: Personalized interactions can lead to more detailed and useful feedback, helping the company improve its offerings.

8. Optimizing Marketing Efforts

Why it Matters:

Effective marketing relies on understanding and meeting the needs of the target audience

How Personalized Interactions Help:

Targeted Marketing: Personalized interactions provide data that can be used for more targeted and effective marketing campaigns.

Increases Relevance: Marketing messages tailored to individual preferences are more likely to resonate and drive conversions.

9. Boosting Employee Satisfaction and Performance

Why it Matters:

Happy and motivated employees are crucial for delivering high-quality customer service.

How Personalized Interactions Help:

Empowers Employees: Employees who can personalize interactions feel more empowered and satisfied in their roles.

Improves Performance: Training employees to personalize service interactions can improve their performance and job satisfaction.

Techniques for Personalizing Interactions:

1. Use Customer Data: Leverage CRM systems and customer databases to access and use customer history, preferences, and purchase patterns.

2. Segment Customers: Group customers based on their behaviors, preferences, and demographics to provide more targeted service.

3. Tailor Communication: Use personalized greetings, messages, and recommendations in all customer communications.

4. Train Employees: Train customer service representatives to recognize opportunities for personalization and equip them with the tools to do so.

5. Follow Up: Send personalized follow-up messages after a purchase or service interaction to show continued care and interest.

Practical Examples of Personalizing Interactions:

Scenario 1: A customer calls for support with a product they frequently purchase.

Personalized Response: "Hi [Customer's Name], I see you've been using our product for a while. How can I assist you with it today?"

Scenario 2: A customer receives a birthday discount.

Personalized Response: "Happy Birthday, [Customer's Name]! Enjoy a 20% discount on your next purchase as a token of our appreciation."

In Conclusion

Personalizing interactions in customer service is a powerful strategy that enhances customer satisfaction, loyalty, and overall experience. By tailoring interactions to individual customer needs and preferences, companies can build stronger relationships, differentiate themselves from competitors, and create positive, memorable customer experiences. Investing in the tools and training needed to personalize service interactions is crucial for any business aiming to provide exceptional customer service.

Seek Feedback

Seeking feedback from customers is a vital aspect of improving customer service. It provides valuable insights into customer perceptions, preferences, and areas where the service might be falling short. Here's a detailed explanation of how seeking feedback helps to improve customer service:

1. Identifying Areas for Improvement

Why it Matters:

Understanding where your service is lacking is the first step in making meaningful improvements.

How Seeking Feedback Helps:

Spotting Weaknesses: Customer feedback highlights specific areas where service can be enhanced, such as response times, communication skills, or product knowledge.

Uncovering Trends: Regular feedback can reveal recurring issues that might not be apparent from isolated incidents.

2. Enhancing Customer Satisfaction

Why it Matters:

Addressing customer concerns and suggestions directly impacts their satisfaction and loyalty.

How Seeking Feedback Helps:

Direct Improvement: Implementing changes based on customer feedback can resolve pain points and enhance the overall customer experience.

Personalized Service: Feedback allows for tailoring services to better meet customer expectations and preferences.

3. Building Customer Trust and Loyalty

Why it Matters:

Customers are more likely to remain loyal to a company that values their input and strives to improve based on their feedback.

How Seeking Feedback Helps:

Shows Commitment: Actively seeking feedback demonstrates a commitment to continuous improvement and customer satisfaction.

Encourages Engagement: Customers who feel their opinions matter are more likely to stay engaged with the brand and return for future business.

4. Preventing Negative Reviews and Churn

Why it Matters:

Unresolved issues can lead to negative reviews and customer churn, damaging the company's reputation and revenue.

How Seeking Feedback Helps:

Early Detection: Feedback can help identify issues before they escalate into larger problems that might result in negative reviews or lost customers.

Proactive Resolution: Acting on feedback promptly shows customers that their concerns are taken seriously, which can prevent dissatisfaction from spreading.

5. Improving Products and Services

Why it Matters:

Customer insights are invaluable for refining products and services to better meet market needs.

How Seeking Feedback Helps:

Innovation: Feedback can inspire new ideas and innovations that enhance the product or service offering.

Quality Assurance: Continuous feedback helps maintain high standards of quality by addressing any defects or shortcomings reported by customers.

6. Enhancing Employee Performance

Why it Matters:

Employee performance directly impacts customer satisfaction.

How Seeking Feedback Helps:

Targeted Training: Feedback can highlight areas where employees need further training or development.

Motivational Tool: Positive feedback can boost employee morale and motivation, while constructive criticism can guide improvement efforts.

7. Creating a Customer-Centric Culture

Why it Matters:

A customer-centric culture prioritizes customer needs and fosters a positive service environment.

How Seeking Feedback Helps:

Aligns Priorities: Regular feedback ensures that the company's focus remains aligned with customer expectations and needs.

Empowers Employees: When employees understand the importance of feedback, they are more likely to adopt a customer-first mindset.

8. Driving Continuous Improvement

Why it Matters:

Customer service should evolve continuously to meet changing customer expectations and market conditions.

How Seeking Feedback Helps:

Informs Strategy: Feedback provides data-driven insights that inform strategic decisions and improvements.

Adapts to Change: Regular feedback helps the company stay agile and responsive to changing customer preferences and market trends.

9. Enhancing Customer Communication

Why it Matters:

Effective communication is crucial for resolving issues and building strong customer relationships.

How Seeking Feedback Helps:

Refines Messaging: Feedback can highlight areas where communication may be unclear or insufficient, allowing for refinement.

Builds Transparency: Seeking feedback and acting on it shows customers that the company values transparency and honest communication.

10. Benchmarking and Competitive Analysis

Why it Matters:

Understanding how your service compares to competitors can provide a competitive edge.

How Seeking Feedback Helps:

Comparative Insights: Feedback can include customer perceptions of how your service compares to competitors, offering insights into areas where you might need to improve.

Market Positioning: Knowing what customers value most can help in positioning your service more effectively in the market.

Techniques for Seeking Feedback:

1. Surveys and Questionnaires: Use online surveys or questionnaires to gather structured feedback from customers.

2. Follow-Up Emails: Send follow-up emails after a purchase or service interaction to request feedback.

3. Social Media Monitoring: Monitor social media channels for customer comments and reviews.

4. Feedback Forms: Provide feedback forms on your website or at the point of sale.

5. Direct Communication: Encourage customer service representatives to ask for feedback during interactions.

6. Customer Interviews: Conduct one-on-one interviews with customers to gather in-depth feedback.

7. Focus Groups: Organize focus groups to discuss specific aspects of your service with a select group of customers.

Implementing Feedback:

- Analyze Data: Regularly analyze feedback data to identify trends and common issues.

- Prioritize Actions: Determine which feedback points are most critical and prioritize actions accordingly.

- Communicate Changes: Inform customers about the changes made based on their feedback, showing that their input has been valued and acted upon.

- Monitor Impact: Continuously monitor the impact of changes to ensure they are achieving the desired improvements.

In Conclusion

Seeking feedback is an essential strategy for improving customer service. It provides invaluable insights into customer needs, preferences, and pain points, allowing companies to make targeted improvements. By actively seeking, analyzing, and implementing customer feedback, businesses can enhance customer satisfaction, build trust and loyalty, prevent negative reviews, and foster a customer-centric culture. Investing in feedback mechanisms and showing a commitment to acting on feedback can significantly elevate the quality of customer service and drive long-term success.

Use Positive Language

Using positive language in customer service is a powerful technique that significantly enhances customer interactions and overall service quality. Positive language involves framing responses in a way that is constructive, optimistic, and solution-focused. Here's a detailed explanation of how using positive language helps to improve customer service:

1. Creating a Positive Customer Experience

Why it Matters:

The tone and wording used in customer interactions greatly influence the customer's perception of the service.

How Positive Language Helps:

Sets a Positive Tone: Positive language sets an upbeat and friendly tone, making customers feel welcome and valued.

Enhances Satisfaction: Customers leave interactions feeling satisfied and positive about the experience, which encourages repeat business.

2. Building Trust and Rapport

Why it Matters:

Building trust and rapport is essential for establishing strong customer relationships.

How Positive Language Helps:

Fosters Connection: Positive, empathetic language helps build a connection with the customer, making them feel understood and respected.

Encourages Openness: When customers feel comfortable and valued, they are more likely to communicate openly, leading to better service outcomes.

3. Improving Communication Clarity

Why it Matters:

Clear communication ensures that customers understand the information being provided and the actions being taken.

How Positive Language Helps:

Avoids Misunderstandings: Positive language minimizes the risk of misunderstandings by clearly conveying information in a friendly and straightforward manner.

Provides Assurance: Using positive language helps reassure customers that their issues are being handled competently and effectively.

4. Enhancing Problem Resolution

Why it Matters:

How problems are communicated and addressed can significantly impact customer satisfaction.

How Positive Language Helps:

Focuses on Solutions: Positive language focuses on what can be done to resolve an issue rather than dwelling on the problem.

Reduces Frustration: Framing responses positively helps reduce customer frustration by emphasizing proactive solutions and next steps.

5. Encouraging Customer Loyalty

Why it Matters:

Positive interactions lead to customer loyalty, which is crucial for long-term business success.

How Positive Language Helps:

Creates Positive Memories: Customers remember positive interactions, which builds loyalty and encourages them to return.

Inspires Advocacy: Satisfied customers are more likely to recommend the company to others, acting as advocates for the brand.

6. Increasing Employee Satisfaction and Performance

Why it Matters:

Employees who use positive language are likely to experience more pleasant interactions, boosting their own job satisfaction and performance.

How Positive Language Helps:

Boosts Morale: Positive interactions with customers can enhance employees' morale and job satisfaction.

Reduces Stress: A positive communication style helps reduce stress for both employees and customers, leading to a more harmonious work environment.

7. Strengthening the Company's Reputation

Why it Matters:

A company's reputation is built on the quality of its customer service.

How Positive Language Helps:

Builds a Positive Image: Consistently using positive language helps build a reputation for excellent, customer-focused service.

Enhances Brand Perception: Customers associate the brand with positive experiences, enhancing overall brand perception.

Techniques for Using Positive Language:

1. Replace Negative Words with Positive Alternatives:

   - Instead of: "I don't know."

   - Use: "Let me find that out for you."

Instead of: "You can't do that."

Use: "What you can do is..."

2. Focus on What You Can Do:

Instead of: "We can't deliver until next week."

Use: "We will ensure delivery by next week."

3. Use Empowering Phrases:

Instead of: "That's not my job."

Use "I'll find someone who can help you with that."

4. Be Specific and Proactive:

Instead of: "I'll try to get this resolved soon."

Use: "I will have this resolved by the end of the day."

5. Express Empathy and Understanding:

Instead of: "Calm down."

Use: "I understand how you feel."

Practical Examples of Positive Language:

Scenario 1: A customer is upset about a delayed shipment.

Negative Response: "I'm sorry, but we can't deliver until next week."

Positive Response: "I understand your frustration. We are working to expedite the delivery and will ensure it reaches you by next week."

Scenario 2: A customer inquires about a product that is out of stock.

Negative Response: "We don't have that in stock."

Positive Response: "That item is very popular! While it's currently out of stock, we expect more next week. Can I notify you as soon as it's available?"

In Conclusion

Using positive language in customer service is a powerful strategy that enhances the customer experience, builds trust, improves communication clarity, and fosters loyalty. By focusing on solutions, showing empathy, and framing responses positively, companies can significantly improve their customer service interactions. Training employees in positive communication techniques and fostering a positive service culture can lead to increased customer satisfaction, stronger relationships, and a better overall reputation for the business.

Be Accessible

Being accessible is a fundamental aspect of excellent customer service. Accessibility in this context refers to ensuring that customers can easily reach and interact with a company through various channels, at their convenience, and receive timely and effective support. Here's a detailed explanation of how being accessible improves customer service:

1. Enhancing Customer Convenience

Why it Matters:

Convenience is a key factor in customer satisfaction. Customers prefer to interact with businesses that are easy to reach and can assist them promptly.

How Being Accessible Helps:

Multiple Channels: Offering various communication channels (phone, email, chat, social media) allows customers to choose their preferred method of contact.

Extended Hours: Providing support outside of regular business hours or offering 24/7 service ensures customers can get help whenever they need it.

2. Improving Response Times

Why it Matters:

Timely responses are critical to resolving issues and meeting customer expectations.

How Being Accessible Helps:

Immediate Assistance: Accessible support channels enable quick responses to customer inquiries and issues, reducing wait times and frustration.

Efficient Issue Resolution: Faster access to support leads to quicker issue resolution, enhancing overall customer satisfaction.

3. Building Customer Trust and Loyalty

Why it Matters:

Trust and loyalty are built when customers feel they can rely on a company to be available and responsive.

How Being Accessible Helps:

Reliability: Consistent availability reassures customers that they can count on the company to be there when needed.

Positive Experience: Easy access to support contributes to a positive customer experience, fostering trust and encouraging repeat business.

4. Facilitating Effective Communication

Why it Matters:

Effective communication is essential for understanding and addressing customer needs and concerns.

How Being Accessible Helps:

Clear Channels: Accessible support channels facilitate clear and effective communication, helping to avoid misunderstandings and ensure accurate information is exchanged.

Responsive Feedback: Accessible communication channels allow for timely feedback and follow-up, ensuring that customers' concerns are addressed promptly.

5. Reducing Customer Frustration

Why it Matters:

Frustration arises when customers encounter barriers to accessing support or resolving issues.

How Being Accessible Helps:

Minimizes Barriers: Easy access to support reduces frustration by removing obstacles that might otherwise impede problem resolution.

Improves Satisfaction: When customers can quickly reach and communicate with support, their overall satisfaction improves, even if the issue is complex.

6. Encouraging Customer Engagement

Why it Matters:

Engagement is key to understanding customer needs and improving service offerings.

How Being Accessible Helps:

Promotes Interaction: Accessible channels encourage customers to engage more frequently, providing valuable insights and feedback.

- **Strengthens Relationships:** Regular interaction through accessible channels helps build stronger relationships and a better understanding of customer preferences.

7. Enhancing Problem-Solving Capabilities

Why it Matters:

Efficient problem-solving relies on the ability to connect with customers and gather relevant information.

How Being Accessible Helps:

Faster Information Gathering Easy access to support allows for quicker collection of information needed to resolve issues.

Effective Solutions: Better access to communication channels improves the ability to provide effective solutions tailored to individual customer needs.

8. Ensuring Inclusivity

Why it Matters:

Inclusivity ensures that all customers, regardless of their preferences or needs, can access support services.

How Being Accessible Helps:

Accommodates Diverse Needs: Offering multiple support channels and ensuring accessibility for people with disabilities (e.g., through accessible websites or customer service lines) ensures that all customers are served effectively.

Broadens Reach: Inclusive practices help reach a wider audience and ensure that all customers have equal access to support.

9. Gathering Valuable Insights

Why it Matters:

Customer interactions provide valuable data that can be used to improve services and products.

How Being Accessible Helps:

Collects Feedback: Accessible channels encourage customers to share their experiences and feedback, providing insights into service performance and areas for improvement.

Monitors Trends: Regular access to customer feedback helps identify trends and patterns that can inform strategic decisions and service enhancements.

10. Supporting Effective Service Recovery

Why it Matters:

Effective recovery from service failures depends on the ability to promptly address customer issues.

How Being Accessible Helps:

Quick Resolution Accessible support channels enable prompt addressing of complaints and issues, aiding in effective service recovery.

Customer Retention: Efficient problem resolution through accessible channels helps retain customers even after service failures, demonstrating commitment to customer satisfaction.

Strategies for Improving Accessibility:

1. Multiple Support Channels: Offer a range of communication options, including phone, email, live chat, social media, and self-service portals.

2. Extended Support Hours: Provide support outside regular business hours or 24/7 to accommodate different time zones and customer schedules.

3. Accessible Technology: Ensure your website and support platforms are accessible to all users, including those with disabilities.

4. Clear Contact Information: Display contact information prominently on your website and other customer touchpoints.

5. Mobile-Friendly Options: Optimize support channels for mobile devices to ensure accessibility for users on smartphones and tablets.

6. Training and Resources: Equip customer service teams with the tools and training needed to manage various support channels effectively.

In Conclusion

Being accessible is a cornerstone of excellent customer service. It enhances customer convenience, improves response times, builds trust and loyalty, and reduces frustration. By ensuring that customers can easily reach and interact with the company through multiple channels, businesses can provide timely support, gather valuable feedback, and foster positive relationships. Investing in accessibility not only improves customer satisfaction but also contributes to a more inclusive and effective service experience.

Follow up

Following up with customers is a critical element of exceptional customer service that significantly enhances the overall customer experience. It involves reaching out to customers after an initial interaction or transaction to ensure their needs have been met, address any lingering issues, and reinforce the relationship. Here's a detailed explanation of how following up helps to improve customer service:

1. **Demonstrating Commitment to Customer Satisfaction**

Why it Matters:

Customers want to feel that their satisfaction is important and that the company values their business.

How Following Up Helps:

Shows Care: Following up demonstrates that the company genuinely cares about the customer's experience and is committed to ensuring their satisfaction.

Builds Trust: Regular follow-ups help build trust by reinforcing the company's commitment to customer service and support.

2. **Ensuring Problem Resolution**

Why it Matters:

Initial interactions may resolve immediate issues, but follow-ups confirm that the solution was effective and that no new problems have arisen.

How Following Up Helps:

Confirms Resolution: Checking in after resolving an issue ensures that the solution worked and that the customer is no longer facing problems.

Prevents Recurrence: Follow-ups provide an opportunity to address any residual concerns and prevent issues from recurring.

3. Enhancing Customer Satisfaction and Loyalty

Why it Matters:

Satisfied customers are more likely to remain loyal and recommend the company to others.

How Following Up Helps:

Reinforces Positive Experience: A well-handled follow-up reinforces a positive customer experience, enhancing overall satisfaction.

Encourages Loyalty: Customers who feel valued and cared for are more likely to become repeat customers and show loyalty to the brand.

4. Gathering Valuable Feedback

Why it Matters:

Feedback provides insights into customer experiences, preferences, and areas for improvement.

How Following Up Helps:

Collects Feedback: Follow-ups provide an opportunity to gather feedback about the customer's experience, offering insights into what worked well and what could be improved.

Identifies Trends: Regular feedback helps identify patterns or recurring issues, enabling the company to make informed improvements.

5. Strengthening Customer Relationships

Why it Matters:

Strong relationships with customers foster trust and encourage continued engagement with the brand.

How Following Up Helps:

Builds Rapport: Personalized follow-ups help build rapport and strengthen the relationship between the customer and the company.

Reinforces Connection: Regular interactions help maintain a connection with customers, making them feel valued and appreciated.

6. Providing Additional Support and Resources

Why it Matters:

Customers may need further assistance or additional information beyond the initial interaction.

How Following Up Helps:

Offers Further Help: Follow-ups provide an opportunity to offer additional support or resources that the customer might need.

Shares Updates: Customers can be informed about new products, services, or updates relevant to their needs.

7. Enhancing Problem-Solving Efficiency

Why it Matters:

Effective problem-solving relies on clear communication and thorough resolution of issues.

How Following Up Helps:

Ensures Clarity: Follow-ups help clarify any remaining doubts or questions the customer may have about the resolution.

Improves Efficiency: Regular follow-ups can lead to more efficient problem-solving by addressing issues comprehensively and promptly.

8. Reducing Negative Reviews and Churn

Why it Matters:

Unresolved issues or poor follow-through can lead to negative reviews and customer churn.

How Following Up Helps:

Prevents Dissatisfaction: Proactive follow-ups can prevent dissatisfaction from escalating into negative reviews or loss of customers.

Mitigates Issues: Addressing concerns promptly through follow-ups helps mitigate potential issues that could lead to customer churn.

9. Demonstrating Professionalism and Reliability

Why it Matters:

Professionalism and reliability are key components of a company's reputation.

How Following Up Helps:

Builds Professional Image: Consistent and timely follow-ups demonstrate professionalism and reliability, enhancing the company's reputation.

Instills Confidence:** Customers feel more confident in a company that follows up and takes responsibility for their experience.

10. Improving Internal Processes

Why it Matters:

Feedback and follow-up interactions can reveal insights into internal processes and areas for improvement.

How Following Up Helps:

Identifies Process Gaps: Follow-up interactions can highlight gaps or inefficiencies in internal processes, leading to improvements.

Informs Training Needs: Feedback from follow-ups can inform training and development needs for customer service teams.

Techniques for Effective Follow-Up:

1. Timely Communication: Follow up within a reasonable timeframe after the initial interaction or transaction to address any outstanding issues.

2. Personalized Approach: Tailor follow-up communication to the specific customer and their previous interactions to make it more relevant and meaningful.

3. Clear Purpose: Ensure that follow-up communication has a clear purpose, whether it's to confirm resolution, gather feedback, or offer additional assistance.

4. Use Multiple Channels: Utilize various communication channels (email, phone, chat) to follow up based on the customer's preferences and previous interactions.

5. Document Interactions: Keep detailed records of follow-up interactions to track progress and ensure consistency in customer service.

Practical Examples of Follow-Up:

Scenario 1: After a customer service issue has been resolved.

Follow-Up Message: "Hi [Customer's Name], I wanted to follow up to ensure that your issue with [specific problem] was resolved to your satisfaction. If you have any further questions or need additional assistance, please let us know."

Scenario 2: After a customer purchase.

Follow-Up Message: "Thank you for your recent purchase, [Customer's Name]. We hope you're enjoying your [product/service]. If you have any feedback or need support, please feel free to reach out."

In Conclusion

Following up is a critical aspect of customer service that enhances satisfaction, builds trust, and strengthens relationships. By demonstrating commitment to customer satisfaction, ensuring problem resolution, and gathering valuable feedback, companies can significantly improve their service quality and customer experience. Effective follow-ups require timely, personalized, and purposeful communication, and they play a crucial role in reinforcing positive customer interactions, preventing issues from escalating, and ultimately fostering long-term customer loyalty.

Empower Employees

Empowering employees is a key strategy for enhancing customer service. It involves giving employees the authority, resources, and confidence to make decisions, solve problems, and provide exceptional service. Here's a detailed explanation of how empowering employees improves customer service:

1. Increases Employee Motivation and Engagement

Why it Matters:

Motivated and engaged employees are more likely to deliver high-quality service and go the extra mile for customers.

How Empowering Employees Helps:

Boosts Morale: When employees are given the autonomy to make decisions and are trusted with responsibilities, their job satisfaction and morale improve.

Enhances Commitment: Empowered employees are more committed to their roles and are likely to show greater enthusiasm in delivering excellent customer service.

2. Enables Faster Problem Resolution

Why it Matters:

Quickly resolving customer issues is crucial for maintaining satisfaction and loyalty.

How Empowering Employees Helps:

Reduces Escalations: By granting employees the authority to handle issues without needing managerial approval, problems can be resolved more swiftly.

Increases Efficiency: Employees who can make decisions on the spot can address customer concerns immediately, leading to faster and more effective problem resolution.

3. Improves Customer Experience

Why it Matters:

A positive customer experience is essential for building strong relationships and encouraging repeat business.

How Empowering Employees Helps:

Personalized Service: Empowered employees can tailor solutions to individual customer needs, providing a more personalized and responsive service.

Proactive Solutions: Employees with the freedom to act can anticipate customer needs and proactively address potential issues before they escalate.

4. Encourages Innovation and Creativity

Why it Matters:

Innovation and creativity contribute to better service offerings and unique customer experiences.

How Empowering Employees Helps:

-Fosters Creativity: Allowing employees to take ownership of their work encourages them to think creatively and come up with innovative solutions.

Promotes Initiative: Employees who feel empowered are more likely to suggest and implement improvements that enhance service quality and customer satisfaction.

5. Builds Trust and Strengthens Relationships

Why it Matters:

Building trust with customers is crucial for fostering long-term relationships and loyalty.

How Empowering Employees Helps:

Demonstrates Trust: Empowering employees signals to customers that the company trusts its staff to handle their needs, which builds trust in the service.

Enhances Relationship: Employees who are empowered to make decisions are better able to build personal connections with customers, strengthening the relationship.

6. Enhances Problem-Solving Skills

Why it Matters:

Effective problem-solving is critical for addressing and resolving customer issues effectively.

How Empowering Employees Helps:

Develops Skills: Empowering employees helps them develop strong problem-solving skills as they handle a variety of situations and challenges independently.

Encourages Learning: Employees who have the autonomy to make decisions learn from their experiences, improving their ability to address future issues effectively.

7. Improves Service Consistency

Why it Matters:

Consistency in service delivery ensures that all customers receive the same high level of service.

How Empowering Employees Helps:

Standardizes Solutions: By providing employees with clear guidelines and the authority to make decisions, service delivery becomes more consistent.

Reduces Variability: Empowered employees are better equipped to handle similar situations in a consistent manner, reducing variability in service quality.

8. Increases Employee Retention

Why it Matters:

High employee turnover can disrupt service quality and negatively impact customer satisfaction.

How Empowering Employees Helps:

Enhances Job Satisfaction: Employees who feel valued and empowered are more likely to stay with the company, reducing turnover and maintaining a stable service team.

Reduces Burnout: Empowerment helps distribute workloads more effectively and reduces burnout by allowing employees to manage their responsibilities more effectively.

9. Strengthens Team Collaboration

Why it Matters:

Effective teamwork is essential for delivering seamless customer service.

How Empowering Employees Helps:

Encourages Collaboration: Empowered employees are more likely to collaborate with their colleagues to solve customer issues and share insights and best practices.

Builds a Supportive Culture: An empowered workforce fosters a supportive and collaborative environment where team members help each other to deliver the best service.

10. Promotes a Customer-Centric Culture

Why it Matters:

A customer-centric culture prioritizes customer needs and fosters a positive service environment.

How Empowering Employees Helps:

Aligns Focus: Empowered employees are more likely to adopt a customer-centric approach, focusing on delivering value and addressing customer needs effectively.

Encourages Ownership: Employees who are given ownership of their roles are more invested in providing exceptional service and ensuring customer satisfaction.

Techniques for Empowering Employees:

1. Provide Training and Resources: Equip employees with the necessary skills, knowledge, and resources to handle customer interactions and make informed decisions.

2. Delegate Authority: Allow employees to make decisions related to customer service without needing constant managerial approval.

3. Encourage Feedback: Create an environment where employees feel comfortable providing feedback and suggestions for improving service.

4. Recognize and Reward: Acknowledge and reward employees for their efforts and successes in delivering outstanding service.

5. Set Clear Guidelines: Establish clear guidelines and boundaries to ensure employees have a framework within which to operate effectively.

6. Foster Open Communication: Encourage open communication between employees and management to support problem-solving and decision-making.

Practical Examples of Empowering Employees:

Scenario 1: A customer is unhappy with a product and requests a refund.

Empowered Response: An employee can immediately process the refund and offer a discount on a future purchase without needing managerial approval.

Scenario 2: A customer has a special request for a product modification.

Empowered Response: An employee can approve the modification request and coordinate with the relevant departments to ensure it is fulfilled.

In Conclusion

Empowering employees is crucial for enhancing customer service. It increases employee motivation and engagement, enables faster problem resolution, and improves the overall customer experience. Empowered employees are more likely to be innovative, build strong relationships with customers, and contribute to a consistent and customer-centric service culture. By providing employees with the authority, resources, and support they need, companies can significantly improve service quality, customer satisfaction, and long-term business success.

Create A Knowledge Base

Creating a knowledge base is a strategic approach to improving customer service by providing a centralized repository of information that both customers and service agents can access. A well-structured knowledge base can streamline operations, enhance the customer experience, and increase overall service efficiency. Here's a detailed explanation of how creating a knowledge base improves customer service:

1. Provides Quick Access to Information

Why it Matters:

Customers and service agents often need quick answers to resolve issues or answer questions.

How a Knowledge Base Helps:

Instant Access: A knowledge base offers instant access to a wide range of information, including FAQs, product details, troubleshooting guides, and company policies.

Reduces Wait Times: By allowing customers to find answers themselves, a knowledge base reduces the time they need to wait for assistance, leading to faster issue resolution.

2. Improves Self-Service Capabilities

Why it Matters:

Customers increasingly prefer to solve problems on their own without contacting support.

How a Knowledge Base Helps:

Empowers Customers: A well-designed knowledge base empowers customers to find solutions and answers on their own, enhancing their self-service experience.

Enhances Convenience: Customers can access the knowledge base at any time, from any device, providing a convenient way to get the information they need without waiting for support.

3. Reduces Support Team Workload

Why it Matters:

A high volume of support requests can overwhelm customer service teams, leading to longer response times and potential burnout.

How a Knowledge Base Helps:

Alleviates Repetitive Queries: By addressing common questions and issues, a knowledge base reduces the number of repetitive inquiries that support agents need to handle.

Streamlines Support: With readily available information, support agents can focus on more complex issues that require human intervention, improving overall efficiency.

4. Ensures Consistent Information

Why it Matters:

Inconsistent information can lead to confusion and dissatisfaction among customers.

How a Knowledge Base Helps:

Standardizes Responses: A centralized knowledge base ensures that all customers and agents access the same accurate and up-to-date information.

Reduces Errors: Consistent information helps reduce errors and discrepancies in responses, leading to a more reliable and trustworthy customer experience.

5. Facilitates Training and Onboarding

Why it Matters:

Effective training and onboarding are crucial for equipping new employees with the knowledge they need to provide excellent service.

How a Knowledge Base Helps:

Provides Training Resources: A knowledge base can serve as a training tool for new employees, offering them a comprehensive overview of products, services, and company procedures.

Supports Ongoing Learning: New hires can refer to the knowledge base as they encounter new scenarios, helping them learn and adapt more quickly.

6. Enhances Problem-Solving Efficiency

Why it Matters:

Quick and efficient problem-solving is essential for maintaining customer satisfaction.

How a Knowledge Base Helps:

Offers Troubleshooting Guides: Detailed troubleshooting guides and step-by-step solutions help both customers and support agents resolve issues more effectively.

Reduces Resolution Time: Access to well-organized information allows support agents to solve problems faster, leading to quicker resolution times.

7. Gathers Valuable Insights

Why it Matters:

Understanding customer needs and issues can help improve products and services.

How a Knowledge Base Helps:

Tracks Usage: Analytics tools within a knowledge base can track which articles are most frequently accessed and what search terms are used.

Identifies Trends: Insights from these analytics can help identify common customer concerns, leading to targeted improvements in products, services, or support content.

8. Supports Multichannel Consistency

Why it Matters:

Customers interact with companies through various channels, and consistency across these channels is important for a seamless experience.

How a Knowledge Base Helps:

Unified Information Source: A knowledge base provides a single source of truth for information, ensuring that responses are consistent across different support channels.

Improves Cross-Channel Support: Whether customers contact support via email, chat, or social media, the knowledge base helps maintain consistent and accurate information.

9. Boosts Customer Confidence and Satisfaction

Why it Matters:

Customers are more satisfied when they can find answers quickly and feel confident about the information they receive.

How a Knowledge Base Helps:

Builds Trust: Providing clear, accurate, and accessible information builds trust and confidence in the company's support.

Enhances Satisfaction: The ability to quickly find solutions or answers improves the overall customer experience, leading to higher satisfaction.

10. Promotes Continuous Improvement

Why it Matters:

Ongoing improvements are essential for keeping the knowledge base relevant and effective.

How a Knowledge Base Helps:

Encourages Updates: Regular updates to the knowledge base ensure that it remains current with the latest information and best practices.

Collects Feedback: Customer and agent feedback on knowledge base articles can highlight areas for improvement and guide updates.

Best Practices for Creating an Effective Knowledge Base:

1. Organize Content Clearly: Structure the knowledge base with a logical hierarchy and easy navigation, using categories and tags to help users find information quickly.

2. Use Simple Language: Write content in clear, straightforward language to ensure that it is easily understood by a broad audience.

3. Include Visuals: Incorporate images, diagrams, and videos to illustrate complex concepts and enhance understanding.

4. Update Regularly: Keep content up-to-date with the latest information, policies, and procedures to ensure accuracy and relevance.

5. Enable Search Functionality: Implement a robust search feature to help users quickly locate specific information or topics.

6. Provide Feedback Mechanisms: Allow users to rate articles and provide feedback to identify areas for improvement and refine content.

Practical Examples of Knowledge Base Utilization:

Scenario 1: A customer has a technical issue with a product.

Knowledge Base Solution: The customer searches the knowledge base and finds a detailed troubleshooting guide that helps resolve the issue without needing to contact support.

Scenario 2: A new employee needs to learn about company procedures.

Knowledge Base Solution: The employee accesses the knowledge base to review onboarding materials, policy documents, and training resources, helping them get up to speed quickly.

In Conclusion

Creating a knowledge base is a powerful tool for improving customer service. It provides quick access to information, supports self-service, reduces support team workload, and ensures consistent and accurate responses. By enhancing problem-solving efficiency, facilitating training, and gathering valuable insights, a well-maintained knowledge base can significantly improve both customer and employee experiences. Adopting best practices and continuously updating the knowledge base ensures its effectiveness and relevance, leading to greater customer satisfaction and more efficient service operations.

Maintain A Positive Attitude

Maintaining a positive attitude is a cornerstone of exceptional customer service. It involves approaching interactions with customers in a cheerful, empathetic, and solution-oriented manner, even when faced with challenges. Here's a detailed explanation of how maintaining a positive attitude improves customer service:

1. Enhances Customer Experience

Why it Matters:

The customer experience is heavily influenced by the demeanor and attitude of service representatives.

How a Positive Attitude Helps:

Creates a Pleasant Interaction: A positive attitude makes interactions more enjoyable for customers, leaving them with a favorable impression of the company.

Builds Rapport: Friendly and upbeat service fosters a connection with customers, making them feel valued and respected.

2. Reduces Customer Frustration

Why it Matters:

Customer frustration can escalate quickly if not managed effectively, especially during challenging interactions.

How a Positive Attitude Helps:

Calms Tensions: A positive demeanor can help de-escalate tense situations by maintaining a calm and reassuring presence.

P-rovides Reassurance: Positive language and attitudes help reassure customers that their issues are being handled with care and attention.

3. Improves Problem-Solving

Why it Matters:

Effective problem-solving requires a proactive and optimistic approach to finding solutions.

How a Positive Attitude Helps:

Encourages Creativity: A positive mindset fosters a solution-oriented approach, encouraging creative and effective solutions to customer problems.

Promotes Persistence: Positivity helps employees remain persistent in resolving issues, even when facing difficult or complex situations.

4. Boosts Employee Morale and Productivity

Why it Matters:

The attitude of customer service employees can impact their own job satisfaction and overall performance.

How a Positive Attitude Helps:

Enhances Job Satisfaction: Employees who maintain a positive attitude are likely to experience higher job satisfaction, which translates into better performance.

Increases Productivity: Positive employees are often more motivated and productive, contributing to more efficient and effective service.

5. Strengthens Customer Loyalty

Why it Matters:

Customer loyalty is often built on the quality of interactions and the overall experience provided.

How a Positive Attitude Helps:

Fosters Trust: A consistently positive interaction helps build trust, leading customers to feel more loyal to the brand.

Encourages Repeat Business: Customers are more likely to return to a company where they have had pleasant and positive interactions.

6. Improves Communication

Why it Matters:

Effective communication is crucial for understanding and addressing customer needs.

How a Positive Attitude Helps:

Facilitates Open Dialogue: A positive approach encourages open and constructive communication, making it easier for customers to express their needs and concerns.

Enhances Clarity: Positive language and attitudes contribute to clearer and more effective communication, reducing misunderstandings.

7. Promotes a Customer-Centric Culture

Why it Matters:

A customer-centric culture prioritizes the needs and satisfaction of customers.

How a Positive Attitude Helps:

Aligns with Company Values: Employees who consistently demonstrate a positive attitude embody the company's commitment to excellent customer service.

Encourages Service Excellence: Positivity reinforces a culture of service excellence, motivating all team members to strive for high standards.

8. Facilitates Effective Conflict Resolution

Why it Matters:

Conflicts and disagreements are inevitable in customer service, and how they are handled can greatly impact customer satisfaction.

How a Positive Attitude Helps:

Maintains Professionalism: A positive attitude helps maintain professionalism during conflicts, ensuring that interactions remain respectful and constructive.

Focuses on Solutions: Positivity encourages a focus on resolving conflicts and finding mutually agreeable solutions, rather than dwelling on the problem.

9. Enhances Team Collaboration

Why it Matters:

Effective teamwork is essential for delivering consistent and high-quality customer service.

How a Positive Attitude Helps:

Builds a Supportive Environment: Positive interactions among team members foster a collaborative and supportive work environment.

Encourages Sharing: A positive attitude encourages team members to share knowledge and best practices, enhancing overall service quality.

10. Creates a Positive Brand Image

Why it Matters:

The impression customers form of a company can influence their perception and future interactions.

How a Positive Attitude Helps:

Reflects Well on the Brand: Employees who maintain a positive attitude contribute to a positive brand image, enhancing the company's reputation.

Attracts New Customers: A strong, positive brand image can attract new customers who are drawn to the company's reputation for excellent service.

Strategies for Maintaining a Positive Attitude:

1. Practice Empathy: Understand and acknowledge the customer's feelings and perspective, which can help maintain a positive and supportive interaction.

2. Use Positive Language: Employ positive and solution-focused language to frame interactions constructively.

3. Stay Calm Under Pressure: Develop techniques for managing stress and remaining composed during challenging situations.

4. Foster a Positive Work Environment: Encourage a supportive and optimistic workplace culture through recognition, team-building activities, and open communication.

5. Invest in Employee Well-being: Provide resources and support to help employees manage stress and maintain a healthy work-life balance.

6. Seek Continuous Improvement: Regularly reflect on interactions and seek feedback to identify areas for maintaining and improving a positive attitude.

Practical Examples of Positive Attitude in Action:

Scenario 1: A customer is frustrated with a delayed order.

Positive Attitude Response: "I understand how frustrating this must be for you, and I'm really sorry for the delay. I'm here to help resolve this as quickly as possible and will keep you updated on the progress."

Scenario 2: A customer makes a special request that is challenging to fulfill.

Positive Attitude Response: "That's a great suggestion, and I'd be happy to look into it further. Let me explore how we can make this happen for you and get back to you with an update soon."

In Conclusion

Maintaining a positive attitude is crucial for improving customer service. It enhances the customer experience, reduces frustration, and boosts problem-solving efficiency. By fostering a positive work environment, improving communication, and strengthening customer loyalty, a positive attitude contributes to overall service excellence. Employees who maintain a positive outlook are better equipped to handle challenges, build strong customer relationships, and contribute to a positive brand image, ultimately leading to higher customer satisfaction and business success.

Offer Proactive support

Offering proactive support is a strategic approach in customer service that focuses on anticipating and addressing customer needs and issues before they become problems. Rather than waiting for customers to reach out with complaints or questions, proactive support involves taking the initiative to provide assistance, guidance, and solutions in advance. Here's a detailed explanation of how offering proactive support improves customer service:

1. Anticipates Customer Needs

Why it Matters:

Understanding and anticipating what customers might need can significantly enhance their experience and satisfaction.

How Proactive Support Helps:

Predicts Issues: By analyzing customer behavior and usage patterns, companies can foresee potential issues and address them before customers encounter them.

Provides Solutions Early: Offering solutions or information before customers ask can prevent issues from arising and improve the overall customer experience.

2. Enhances Customer Satisfaction

Why it Matters:

Customer satisfaction is closely linked to how well their needs are anticipated and met.

How Proactive Support Helps:

Surprises and Delights: Proactive support can pleasantly surprise customers, as they appreciate when a company takes the initiative to help them without being prompted.

Reduces Frustration: By addressing potential issues before they become problems, proactive support reduces customer frustration and enhances overall satisfaction.

3. Improves Problem Resolution Efficiency

Why it Matters:

Efficient problem resolution is crucial for maintaining customer trust and loyalty.

How Proactive Support Helps:

Prevents Escalations: By identifying and addressing issues early, proactive support prevents them from escalating into more significant problems that require complex solutions.

Streamlines Processes: Addressing potential issues in advance helps streamline support processes, as solutions are implemented before customers even experience the problem.

4. Builds Stronger Customer Relationships

Why it Matters:

Strong customer relationships are built on trust, reliability, and understanding.

How Proactive Support Helps:

Shows Care: Proactively reaching out to customers demonstrates that the company is attentive to their needs and values their business.

Builds Trust: Customers are more likely to trust and remain loyal to a company that consistently anticipates and addresses their needs.

5. Reduces the Volume of Reactive Support Requests

Why it Matters:

High volumes of reactive support requests can strain resources and impact service quality.

How Proactive Support Helps:

Decreases Support Load: By addressing issues before they arise, proactive support reduces the number of reactive support requests that need to be handled.

Enhances Efficiency: With fewer reactive requests, support teams can focus on providing higher-quality service and resolving more complex issues.

6. Fosters Customer Loyalty

Why it Matters:

Customer loyalty is crucial for long-term business success and repeat business.

How Proactive Support Helps:

Encourages Repeat Business: Customers who experience proactive support are more likely to return and continue doing business with the company.

Promotes Advocacy: Satisfied customers who feel valued are more likely to recommend the company to others, enhancing brand reputation and attracting new customers.

7. Provides Valuable Insights

Why it Matters:

Understanding customer needs and issues helps improve products and services.

How Proactive Support Helps:

Gathers Data: Proactive support interactions provide valuable data on customer behavior and potential issues, helping companies refine their offerings.

Informs Improvements: Insights from proactive support can guide product development, service enhancements, and strategic decision-making.

8. Enhances Brand Reputation

Why it Matters:

A strong brand reputation is built on consistent and positive customer experiences.

How Proactive Support Helps:

Strengthens Image: Companies known for offering proactive support are seen as forward-thinking and customer-centric, enhancing their reputation.

Differentiates from Competitors: Proactive support sets a company apart from competitors who may only provide reactive service, attracting and retaining customers.

9. Improves Employee Morale

Why it Matters:

Employee satisfaction and morale can impact the quality of customer service.

How Proactive Support Helps:

Reduces Stress: Proactive support can reduce the stress and pressure on support teams by preventing issues from escalating and requiring emergency intervention.

Boosts Job Satisfaction: Employees who are empowered to provide proactive support often experience greater job satisfaction, as they can deliver high-quality service and make a positive impact.

10. Supports Long-Term Customer Engagement

Why it Matters:

Ongoing engagement with customers fosters loyalty and long-term relationships.

How Proactive Support Helps:

Encourages Engagement: Proactive support creates opportunities for ongoing engagement by regularly providing value and addressing needs before they arise.

Builds Loyalty: Consistent proactive interactions help maintain customer engagement and foster long-term loyalty.

Strategies for Implementing Proactive Support:

1. Analyze Customer Data: Use analytics tools to identify common issues, trends, and customer behaviors that can inform proactive support initiatives.

2. Create Knowledge Resources: Develop and maintain resources such as FAQs, guides, and tutorials to address common questions and issues before they arise.

3. Monitor Product Usage: Track how customers use products or services to identify potential problems and offer solutions before issues are reported.

4. Implement Automated Alerts: Set up automated systems to notify customers of potential issues, updates, or changes that may impact them.

5. Engage in Regular Communication: Reach out to customers with updates, tips, and offers that are relevant to their needs and usage patterns.

6. Train Support Teams: Equip support teams with the skills and tools needed to anticipate customer needs and provide proactive assistance.

Practical Examples of Proactive Support:

Scenario 1: A software company identifies a common issue that users experience during a particular update.

Proactive Support Action: The company sends out a preemptive communication to all users with instructions on how to avoid the issue and offers resources for troubleshooting.

Scenario 2: An online retailer notices that many customers are frequently inquiring about the status of their orders.

Proactive Support Action: The retailer implements automated order tracking updates and sends regular notifications to customers about their order status.

In Conclusion

Offering proactive support significantly enhances customer service by anticipating and addressing customer needs before they become problems. It improves customer satisfaction, reduces support workload, builds stronger relationships, and enhances brand reputation. By implementing strategies such as analyzing customer data, creating knowledge resources, and engaging in regular communication, companies can effectively deliver proactive support and create a more positive and efficient customer experience.

Show Appreciation

Showing appreciation is a powerful and often underutilized tactic in customer service that can significantly enhance customer satisfaction and loyalty. When customers feel valued and recognized, they are more likely to continue their relationship with a company and recommend it to others. Here's a detailed explanation of how showing appreciation improves customer service:

1. Strengthens Customer Loyalty

Why it Matters:

Loyal customers are more likely to make repeat purchases and provide positive word-of-mouth referrals.

How Showing Appreciation Helps:

Reinforces Connection: Regularly expressing gratitude reinforces the emotional connection customers have with the brand, making them feel valued and appreciated.

Encourages Repeat Business: Customers who feel appreciated are more inclined to return and continue their relationship with the company.

2. Enhances Customer Satisfaction

Why it Matters:

Customer satisfaction is directly linked to the overall experience they have with a company.

How Showing Appreciation Helps:

Increases Positivity: When customers are acknowledged for their business or feedback, it enhances their overall experience and satisfaction.

Creates Positive Experiences: Appreciation contributes to a positive experience, making customers more likely to view their interactions with the company favorably.

3. **Builds Stronger Relationships**

Why it Matters:

Strong relationships with customers foster trust and long-term engagement.

How Showing Appreciation Helps:

Builds Trust: By showing genuine appreciation, companies build trust with their customers, demonstrating that they value and respect their patronage.

Fosters Personal Connections: Personalized expressions of gratitude, such as thank-you notes or recognition of customer milestones, help build deeper connections with customers.

4. **Encourages Customer Advocacy**

Why it Matters:

Customers who feel appreciated are more likely to advocate for the brand and share their positive experiences with others.

How Showing Appreciation Helps:

Promotes Referrals: Satisfied customers who feel valued are more likely to recommend the company to friends, family, and colleagues.

Generates Positive Reviews: Customers who receive appreciation are more inclined to leave positive reviews and feedback, enhancing the company's reputation.

5. Differentiates from Competitors

Why it Matters:

In a competitive market, standing out can be crucial for attracting and retaining customers.

How Showing Appreciation Helps:

Creates a Competitive Edge: Companies that consistently show appreciation differentiate themselves from competitors who may not prioritize customer recognition.

Enhances Brand Image: A reputation for valuing and appreciating customers strengthens the brand's image and appeal.

6. Increases Employee Morale

Why it Matters:

Happy and motivated employees are essential for delivering excellent customer service.

How Showing Appreciation Helps:

Boosts Motivation: Employees who see the positive impact of appreciation on customer satisfaction are more motivated to maintain high service standards.

Improves Job Satisfaction: Acknowledging employees' efforts in showing appreciation to customers can lead to increased job satisfaction and morale.

7. Encourages Customer Feedback

Why it Matters:

Customer feedback is valuable for improving products, services, and overall customer experience.

How Showing Appreciation Helps:

Promotes Openness: Customers who feel appreciated are more likely to provide honest feedback and suggestions for improvement.

Enhances Engagement: Expressing gratitude for feedback encourages customers to continue sharing their thoughts and opinions.

8. Facilitates Conflict Resolution

Why it Matters:

Effectively handling conflicts and complaints is critical for maintaining positive customer relationships.

How Showing Appreciation Helps:

Mitigates Negative Feelings: Showing appreciation during conflict resolution helps to alleviate negative feelings and demonstrates a commitment to customer satisfaction.

Fosters Positive Outcomes: Acknowledging and valuing the customer's concerns can lead to more positive and constructive outcomes during conflict resolution.

9. Promotes a Positive Service Culture

Why it Matters:

A positive service culture supports consistent and high-quality customer interactions.

How Showing Appreciation Helps:

Reinforces Service Standards: Regularly showing appreciation reinforces a culture of respect and consideration, leading to consistent high-quality service.

Encourages Positive Behavior: Employees who observe and participate in a culture of appreciation are more likely to adopt and maintain positive service behaviors.

10. Improves Customer Retention

Why it Matters:

Retaining existing customers is often more cost-effective than acquiring new ones.

How Showing Appreciation Helps:

Increases Retention Rates: Customers who feel appreciated are more likely to stay loyal to the company and continue their business relationship.

Reduces Churn: By consistently acknowledging and valuing customers, companies can reduce the likelihood of churn and retain their customer base.

Techniques for Showing Appreciation:

1. Personalized Thank-You Notes: Send personalized thank-you notes or emails to customers to acknowledge their business and express gratitude.

2. Special Offers and Discounts: Provide special offers, discounts, or rewards to customers as a token of appreciation for their loyalty.

3. Recognition Programs: Implement customer recognition programs that celebrate milestones, such as anniversaries or significant purchases.

4. Exclusive Access: Offer exclusive access to new products, services, or events as a way to show appreciation for loyal customers.

5. Public Acknowledgment: Recognize customers publicly through social media shout-outs, testimonials, or featured stories to highlight their importance.

6. Follow-Up Communication: Reach out to customers after their purchase or interaction to thank them and check on their satisfaction.

Practical Examples of Showing Appreciation:

Scenario 1: A customer has made several purchases over the years.

Appreciation Action: Send a personalized thank-you note with a discount on their next purchase and express gratitude for their continued support.

Scenario 2: A customer provides valuable feedback on a recent product experience.

Appreciation Action: Thank the customer for their feedback, acknowledge the impact of their input, and offer a small gift or discount as a token of appreciation.

In Conclusion

Showing appreciation is a vital aspect of improving customer service. It strengthens customer loyalty, enhances satisfaction, and builds stronger relationships. By encouraging customer advocacy, differentiating from competitors, and increasing employee morale, appreciation contributes to a positive service culture and improves overall customer retention. Implementing techniques such as personalized thank-you notes, special offers, and recognition programs helps create meaningful interactions that value and acknowledge customers, ultimately leading to a more positive and successful customer service experience.

Handle Complaints Gracefully

Handling complaints gracefully is a crucial component of excellent customer service. When executed effectively, it can turn a potentially negative experience into a positive one, enhancing customer satisfaction and loyalty. Here's a detailed explanation of how handling complaints gracefully improves customer service:

1. Demonstrates Commitment to Customer Satisfaction

Why it Matters:

Customers need to feel that their concerns are taken seriously and that the company is committed to addressing their issues.

How Handling Complaints Gracefully Helps:

Builds Trust: By addressing complaints with empathy and efficiency, companies show that they value customer feedback and are dedicated to resolving issues.

Strengthens Relationships: A graceful handling of complaints can strengthen the customer relationship, showing that the company is invested in their satisfaction.

2. Reduces Customer Frustration

Why it Matters:

Unresolved complaints can escalate customer frustration and negatively impact their perception of the company.

How Handling Complaints Gracefully Helps:

Alleviates Anger: Calm and empathetic responses help diffuse frustration and prevent the situation from escalating further.

Offers Reassurance: Providing clear solutions and timely updates reassures customers that their concerns are being addressed effectively.

3. Enhances Customer Retention

Why it Matters:

Retaining customers is often more cost-effective than acquiring new ones, and effectively managing complaints is key to retention.

How Handling Complaints Gracefully Helps:

Increases Loyalty: Customers who experience satisfactory resolutions to their complaints are more likely to remain loyal to the company.

Encourages Repeat Business: Effective resolution of complaints can lead to increased customer retention and repeat business.

4. Provides Valuable Feedback for Improvement

Why it Matters:

Complaints can offer insights into areas where products, services, or processes may need improvement.

How Handling Complaints Gracefully Helps:

Identifies Issues: Gracefully managing complaints often uncovers recurring issues or systemic problems that can be addressed to enhance overall quality.

Guides Enhancements: Constructive feedback from complaints can guide improvements and innovations, leading to a better customer experience.

5. Enhances Brand Reputation

Why it Matters:

A company's reputation is shaped by how it handles customer interactions, including complaints.

How Handling Complaints Gracefully Helps:

Builds a Positive Image: Companies that handle complaints effectively are perceived as reliable and customer-centric, enhancing their overall brand reputation.

Generates Positive Reviews: Satisfied customers who see their complaints addressed gracefully are more likely to leave positive reviews and testimonials.

6. Promotes a Positive Service Culture

Why it Matters:

A positive service culture supports high-quality interactions and overall customer satisfaction.

How Handling Complaints Gracefully Helps:

Encourages Best Practices: Handling complaints gracefully sets a standard for how all customer interactions should be managed, promoting a culture of empathy and respect.

Empowers Employees: Employees who are trained and encouraged to handle complaints effectively contribute to a supportive and customer-focused environment.

7. Facilitates Effective Conflict Resolution

Why it Matters:

Conflicts are inevitable, and effectively managing them is essential for maintaining positive relationships.

How Handling Complaints Gracefully Helps:

Resolves Issues Constructively: A graceful approach to complaints involves active listening and problem-solving, leading to constructive resolutions.

Maintains Professionalism: Handling complaints professionally helps ensure that conflicts are resolved respectfully and efficiently.

8. Improves Communication Skills

Why it Matters:

Effective communication is crucial for understanding and addressing customer needs.

How Handling Complaints Gracefully Helps:

Enhances Clarity: Graceful handling of complaints involves clear, transparent communication, which helps ensure that customers understand the resolution process.

Fosters Openness: Encouraging open dialogue during complaint resolution helps build trust and ensures that all concerns are addressed.

9. Encourages Customer Feedback

Why it Matters:

Encouraging feedback helps companies understand customer experiences and identify areas for improvement.

How Handling Complaints Gracefully Helps:

Promotes Feedback Sharing: Customers are more likely to provide honest feedback when they feel their complaints are handled with respect and seriousness.

Builds a Feedback Loop: An effective complaint resolution process creates a feedback loop that informs ongoing improvements and enhancements.

10. Demonstrates Company Values

Why it Matters:

Company values and principles should be reflected in all customer interactions.

How Handling Complaints Gracefully Helps:

Reflects Integrity: Gracefully managing complaints demonstrates a company's commitment to integrity, respect, and customer care.

Reinforces Core Values: Effective complaint handling reinforces the company's core values and commitment to providing excellent customer service.

Strategies for Handling Complaints Gracefully:

1. Listen Actively: Give the customer your full attention, listen to their concerns without interrupting, and acknowledge their feelings.

2. Show Empathy: Express understanding and empathy for the customer's situation, validating their experience and emotions.

3. Apologize Sincerely: Offer a genuine apology for the inconvenience or issue, even if the problem was not directly caused by the company.

4. Offer Solutions: Provide clear, actionable solutions to address the complaint, and ensure that the customer understands the steps being taken.

5. Follow Up: Check back with the customer to ensure that the resolution met their expectations and to demonstrate continued care and attention.

6. Train Employees: Provide training for employees on effective complaint handling techniques, including communication skills, empathy, and problem-solving.

7. Document Complaints: Keep detailed records of complaints and resolutions to identify trends, track performance, and inform future improvements.

Practical Examples of Graceful Complaint Handling:

Scenario 1: A customer receives a damaged product.

Graceful Handling Action: Apologize for the inconvenience, offer a replacement or refund, and ensure that the customer is satisfied with the resolution.

Scenario 2: A customer experiences long wait times for support.

Graceful Handling Action: Acknowledge the delay, apologize for the inconvenience, and provide a discount or compensation as a gesture of goodwill, along with steps to improve wait times in the future.

In Conclusion

Handling complaints gracefully is essential for delivering exceptional customer service. It demonstrates a commitment to customer satisfaction, reduces frustration, and strengthens customer relationships. By providing constructive resolutions, improving communication, and reflecting company values, graceful complaint handling enhances brand reputation and fosters a positive service culture. Implementing strategies such as active listening, empathy, and sincere apologies helps companies manage complaints effectively and turn challenging situations into opportunities for customer engagement and improvement.

www.ingramcontent.com/pod-product-compliance
Lightning Source LLC
Chambersburg PA
CBHW071937210526
45479CB00002B/721